AMAZING DECADES IN PHOTOS

THE 1990s
DECADE IN PHOTOS
THE RISE OF TECHNOLOGY

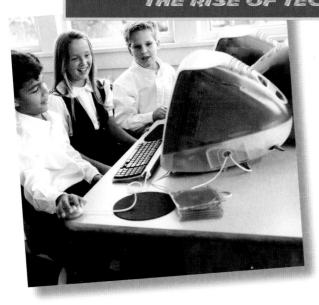

Jim Corrigan

Enslow Publishers, Inc.
40 Industrial Road
Box 398
Berkeley Heights, NJ 07922
USA

http://www.enslow.com

Library of Congress Cataloging-in-Publication Data

Corrigan, Jim.
    The 1990s decade in photos : the rise of technology / by Jim Corrigan.
        p. cm. — (Amazing decades in photos)
    Includes bibliographical references and index.
    Summary: "Middle school readers will find out about the important world, national, and cultural developments of the decade 1990–1999"—Provided by publisher.
    ISBN-13: 978-0-7660-3138-8 (alk. paper)
    ISBN-10: 0-7660-3138-1 (alk. paper)
    1. United States—History—1961—Pictorial works—Juvenile literature. 2. United States—Social conditions—1980—Pictorial works—Juvenile literature. 3. History, Modern—1989—-Pictorial works—Juvenile literature. 4. Nineteen nineties—Pictorial works—Juvenile literature. I. Title.
    E881.C67 2009
    973.92—dc22

                                                                                      2008054648

Printed in the United States of America.

092009 Lake Book Manufacturing, Inc., Melrose Park, IL

10 9 8 7 6 5 4 3 2 1

Produced by OTTN Publishing, Stockton, N.J.

TABLE OF CONTENTS

The flag of the Russian Federation flies over the Kremlin, the country's central government complex. In December 1991 the Soviet Union broke up into Russia and fourteen other independent states. This left the United States as the world's only superpower.

WELCOME TO THE 1990s

*T*he 1990s were a time of new inventions. During the twentieth century, technology developed faster than ever before. People welcomed amazing inventions such as the airplane and television. During the century's second half, computers emerged. They were a powerful new technology. By the 1990s, computers were the gateway to important new discoveries.

In September 1993, a new era of peace in the Middle East seemed possible. U.S. president Bill Clinton brought Israel's prime minister Yitzhak Rabin and Palestinian leader Yasir Arafat to the White House to sign a peace accord. Unfortunately, Israel and the Palestinians could not reach a permanent agreement, and the peace collapsed into violence in the fall of 2000.

Not everyone was happy about new technology. A man known as the Unabomber sent bombs through the mail, killing three people and wounding many others, to protest what he considered the problems of modern industrial society. In April 1996, FBI agents arrested the Unabomber (center), whose real name was Theodore Kaczynski. He was sentenced to life in prison for his crimes.

With computers, scientists studied the blueprints of life. They began the Human Genome Project in 1990. This was a massive effort to learn how the human body grows and develops. A few years later, scientists discovered a way to clone animals. They made an exact copy of a sheep. New technology also aided the study of space. In 1990, the Hubble Space Telescope was launched into orbit. It offered amazing views of the universe. In 1997, a tiny rover roamed the surface of Mars. It sent back stunning images of the Red Planet.

Meanwhile, people were just starting to use the Internet during the 1990s. This global computer network quickly became part of everyday life. E-mail, web browsers, and search engines were powerful new tools. They made it easy to find information and talk with others. Students did research online. Shoppers bought items from home instead of going to a store. People could make new friends in faraway places. The Internet changed society.

New technology could not solve all of the world's problems, however. In some cases, it added to them. The Internet enabled thieves to commit crimes online. People debated the potential risks of cloning animals. As the decade closed, people worried that a potential computer glitch called Y2K might bring disaster to our technology-driven society.

Some of humanity's most ancient problems also remained. Medicine had made great strides, but fatal illnesses still existed. The deadly disease HIV/AIDS ravaged Africa during the 1990s. Conflicts still plagued the world as well. In the Middle East, Iraq invaded Kuwait during the summer of 1990. Troops from across the globe united to free the tiny kingdom in early 1991. Later in the decade, a new group of terrorists gained strength. Their organization, known as al-Qaeda, began a war of terror against the United States and its allies.

Foreign terrorists were not the only threat. In 1995, a U.S. citizen blew up a government building in Oklahoma. Four years later, two high school students went on a deadly rampage in Colorado. They killed thirteen classmates and teachers before taking their own lives. Americans struggled to understand the reasons for these dreadful acts. Even larger massacres were taking place in other parts of the world. In Bosnia and Rwanda, enormous groups of people were killed because of ethnic differences.

As the final decade of the twentieth century ended, people looked to the future. Technology promised more great discoveries. Computers were becoming smaller and faster. There would be many new uses for them. Yet technology also promised more challenges. It rushed the pace of life. It made families and friends more isolated from each other. The 1990s showed that technology had benefits and drawbacks.

Bill Clinton's presidency was beset by many scandals. These protesters are calling for the president to be impeached, or removed from office. In December 1998, the U.S. House of Representatives officially charged Clinton with several crimes. However, in February 1999 the U.S. Senate determined that Clinton was not guilty of the charges, and the president was permitted to remain in office.

An American M-1 Abrams tank rolls into battle against Iraqi forces, 1991. Soldiers from the United States and many other countries worked together to defeat Iraq in the Gulf War.

Nations Rally to Free Kuwait

Kuwait is a tiny, oil-rich country in the Middle East. Iraq and Saudi Arabia are its neighbors. In 1990, Iraq suddenly attacked Kuwait. Iraqi soldiers overran the country. The invasion started a war. More than thirty nations joined to free Kuwait. The conflict came to be known as the Gulf War.

Iraq invaded Kuwait because it needed money. During the 1980s, Iraq had waged a long and costly war against Iran. The war left Iraq's economy ruined. Iraqi leader Saddam Hussein looked to Kuwait for help. He argued that Iraq had fought to protect other Arab countries from Iran. Saddam demanded that wealthy Kuwait pay some of Iraq's debts.

Iraq's conquest of Kuwait gave dictator Saddam Hussein (1937-2006) control of about 40 percent of the world's oil supply. This posed a serious threat to the United States, Japan, and the countries of Western Europe. These highly industrialized nations depended on oil to keep their economies running smoothly.

When Kuwait refused, Saddam Hussein became hostile. He claimed that Kuwait was stealing Iraqi oil. He also said that, historically, Kuwait had been part of Iraq. In August 1990, Iraqi troops and tanks rolled into Kuwait. They crushed Kuwait's small army. Many Kuwaiti citizens fled. Others were taken prisoner. Countries around the world were outraged. They demanded that the Iraqi forces leave immediately. But a defiant Saddam Hussein said that Kuwait now belonged to his nation.

Saudi Arabia feared that it too might be attacked by Iraq. The Saudi government asked for help from other nations. More than 600,000 troops from around the world went to Saudi Arabia. The United States sent the most soldiers. It led the partnership, or coalition, of countries. The mission to protect Saudi Arabia was dubbed Operation Desert Shield.

A few days after Iraq's invasion of Kuwait, U.S. troops were sent to Saudi Arabia. They established bases from which coalition troops would launch Operation Desert Storm in January 1991.

American General Norman Schwarzkopf (left) and other coalition leaders discuss cease-fire terms with Iraqi generals, February 1991.

Once Saudi Arabia was safe, the coalition looked to free Kuwait. This part of the mission was named Operation Desert Storm. Before attacking, the coalition gave Iraq a chance to leave Kuwait peacefully. Saddam Hussein refused. In January 1991, coalition airplanes began bombing the Iraqi troops. Deadly air strikes continued for over a month. Then the coalition ground forces attacked. They defeated the Iraqis in just 100 hours of fighting. Kuwait was once again free.

Upon achieving their goal, most of the coalition soldiers went home. Some stayed behind to ensure that Iraq did not threaten Kuwait or Saudi Arabia again. Members of the United Nations agreed that Iraq should give up its programs to create weapons of mass destruction (WMD), such as nuclear bombs or chemical weapons. However, despite the defeat, Saddam Hussein remained in power. Throughout the 1990s, the United States and its allies continued to watch Iraq. They were prepared to intervene with military force if Iraq attacked its neighbor again.

RACE RIOTS ROCK LOS ANGELES

A riot is a sudden and violent uprising by a mob. Those who take part in a riot are usually angry about something. In 1992, a huge riot rocked the city of Los Angeles. The rioters destroyed homes and businesses, causing more than a billion dollars in damage.

A court case sparked the Los Angeles riot. Four white police officers were on trial for beating a black suspect named Rodney King. In March 1991, King had led the police on a high-speed car chase. Once caught, he resisted arrest. The police officers shot him twice with an electric "stun gun." They punched and kicked him, and they kept hitting King even after he was on the ground. A witness captured part of the incident on videotape. The video aired on TV all across the country.

In April 1992, a jury made up of ten whites, one Hispanic, and one Asian found the police officers not guilty. African American and Latino residents of Los Angeles were furious. Thousands stormed the streets. They attacked innocent bystanders. They started fires and looted stores. Street gangs added to the mayhem. The rioting lasted for almost a week. Finally, soldiers helped police halt the violence.

A man named George Holliday took this video of Los Angeles police officers beating Rodney King, March 6, 1991.

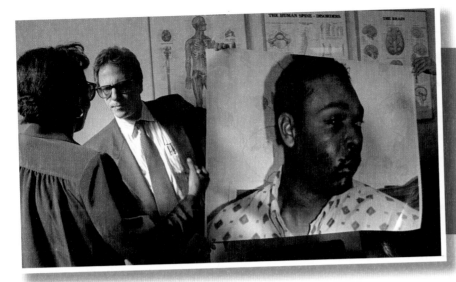

More than 50 people died during the rioting in Los Angeles. Another 2,300 were seriously injured. Some of the rioters who broke laws were later arrested, but many avoided punishment.

In 1993, the four police officers involved in the beating of Rodney King were again put on trial. This time they were charged with the federal crime of violating King's civil rights. Two of the officers were acquitted. The other two were found guilty. They were sentenced to prison terms of two and a half years.

A fire department crew sprays water on a burning mini-mall in south Los Angeles, April 30, 1992. The building was one of many set on fire during a night of rioting.

BILL CLINTON IS ELECTED PRESIDENT

In 1992, President George H. W. Bush ran for reelection. He faced two opponents: Bill Clinton and Ross Perot. The Democratic Party candidate, Clinton, was the longtime governor of Arkansas. Perot was a wealthy businessman from Texas. He ran as an independent candidate to challenge the Republicans and Democrats. As the November election neared, each candidate worked hard to attract voters.

Independent challenger Ross Perot, Democratic Party candidate Bill Clinton, and Republican president George Bush face a panel of reporters during the first public debate of the 1992 presidential campaign.

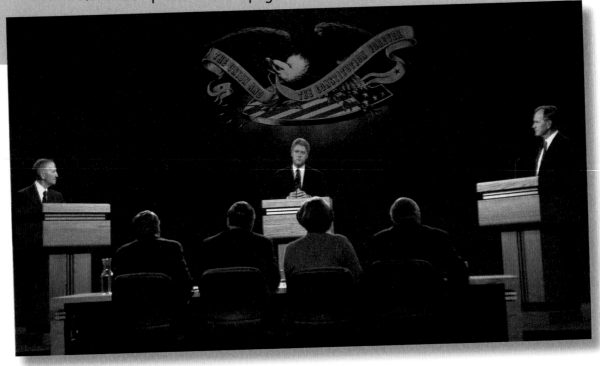

With his wife Hillary and daughter Chelsea at his side, William Jefferson Clinton takes the oath of office as the nation's forty-second president.

At first, President Bush appeared likely to win. People admired his role in winning the Gulf War. Bush had brought together the coalition of nations that freed Kuwait. The feat seemed to ensure him of another term as president. However, there was a problem. The U.S. economy was weak. Companies were going out of business, and many Americans were worried about their jobs.

Clinton and Perot said that President Bush was responsible for the weak economy. They said that the president did not care about workers. They also noted that Bush had broken a 1988 pledge not to raise taxes. Both candidates promised to improve the economy if elected.

On Election Day, Bill Clinton soundly defeated President Bush. Ross Perot finished a distant third.

Bomb Explodes in World Trade Center

*T*he twin towers of the World Trade Center dominated New York City's skyline. They were the tallest buildings in the city. They were also a symbol of America's business strength. In 1993, terrorists tried to destroy the towers with a bomb.

The attack came on February 26, 1993. A young man drove to the World Trade Center in a rented van. His name was Ramzi Yousef. He parked the van in an underground garage. The van held an enormous bomb. Yousef thought that the explosion would be powerful enough to topple the towers above.

Yousef was wrong. The explosion ripped through six floors. It killed six people and

In 1993, the twin towers of the World Trade Center (right) were the tallest buildings in New York. They rose more than a hundred stories above the streets of lower Manhattan.

The explosion beneath the World Trade Center tore a massive crater in the lower floors of the north tower.

injured more than a thousand. Yet the twin towers did not fall. Americans were shocked by the deadly attack.

Ramzi Yousef and others involved in the bombing were later caught. They had links to a terrorist group from the Middle East. The group called itself al-Qaeda.

In 1993, few people had heard of al-Qaeda. Less than a decade later, everyone would know about the terrorist organization. The group had declared war on the United States. The World Trade Center bombing of 1993 was the first time al-Qaeda was involved in a large attack against a U.S. target. In the years ahead, al-Qaeda would strike many more times. The attacks would grow ever more deadly. On September 11, 2001, al-Qaeda achieved its goal of destroying the twin towers when terrorists flew airplanes into the buildings.

THE MYSTERY OF GENES

Genes are the blueprints of life. We each carry a full set of genes in our body's cells. The genes describe everything about us. They determine our hair color, eye color, height, and more. During the 1990s, scientists made great leaps forward in understanding genes.

In 1990, U.S. scientists started the Human Genome Project. This was a bold effort to identify every type of human gene. Scientists from many other nations soon joined the project. It took thirteen years of hard work, but they succeeded. Scientists found that there are nearly 25,000 genes in a human cell. Currently, genetic research is leading to new treatments for many diseases.

Cloning is the act of making an exact copy of something. In 1996, Scottish scientists learned how to clone animals. They took the genes of an adult sheep

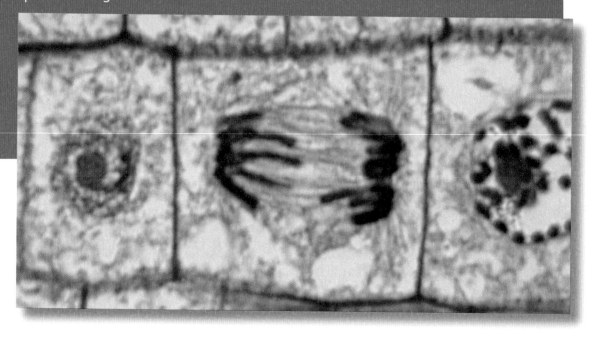

This microscope view shows chromosomes—the tiny structures that contain a person's full genetic code—in a human cell that is about to divide.

Dr. Ian Wilmut sits with Dolly the cloned sheep in Edinburgh, Scotland, March 1996. Dr. Wilmut supervised the cloning program at the Roslin Institute in Scotland during the mid-1990s.

and copied them to make a genetically identical sheep. They named the new sheep Dolly. She was an amazing feat of science. Scientists have since cloned other animals, such as cows, pigs, and rabbits. However, the clones are not as healthy as the original animals.

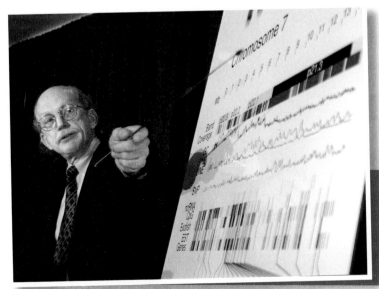

Human cloning is not yet possible. But scientists believe it will be possible in the future. Most people are opposed to the idea of ever cloning a human. They warn about the dangers of meddling with nature.

Dr. Robert Waterston of the Washington University Genome Sequencing Center discusses DNA and genetics at a press conference.

The Mystery of Genes

Nelson Mandela, president of the African National Congress (ANC), casts his ballot in his country's first election open to all races, April 1994. This historic election marked the end of apartheid in South Africa.

AN END TO APARTHEID

South Africa is a country at the southern tip of the African continent. Four out of five people who live there are black. For most of the twentieth century, South Africa's white minority ruled the country. They used an unfair system of laws called *apartheid*. Apartheid kept blacks and whites separate. White people had better jobs, finer homes, and much more freedom.

This sign marks a "whites only" beach near Cape Town. In South Africa during the apartheid era, whites and blacks were segregated.

Blacks in South Africa had been treated unfairly for a long time. But in 1948, apartheid became the government's official policy. South Africans were separated into three groups: whites, blacks, and colored (people of mixed descent). The laws gave whites every advantage. They lived in the best neighborhoods. They earned more money at work. Their children received a better education. Meanwhile, nonwhites lived in poverty. They labored under harsh rules.

From the beginning, black South Africans opposed apartheid. At first, they staged peaceful protests and strikes. In 1960, the struggle against apartheid turned deadly. A large crowd gathered in the town of Sharpeville to protest apartheid. The crowd surrounded the police station. The situation grew tense. After some protesters threw rocks, the white police officers opened fire. They continued shooting even after the protesters began running away. Sixty-nine people were killed, and 180 more were injured.

Coffins, representing blacks killed by South African police, are carried in this parade on the twenty-fifth anniversary of the 1960 Sharpeville massacre. The March 21 massacre is remembered each year as the International Day for the Elimination of Racial Discrimination.

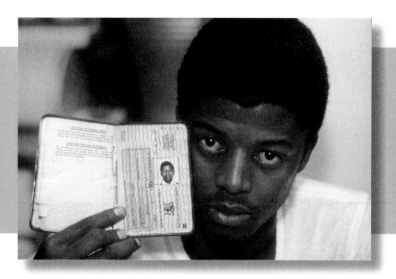

A South African man shows his government-issued passbook. Under apartheid, blacks were required to carry these documents, which said where the person was permitted to live, work, and travel. Such restrictions did not apply to white South Africans, however.

The Sharpeville massacre was a turning point in South African history. Black groups began using violence to end apartheid. Other countries began criticizing South Africa's unfair laws. For decades, the white government rejected all calls to change apartheid. Instead, it cracked down on black political groups. Leaders were thrown in jail.

During the late 1980s, pressure to end apartheid increased. Riots erupted on South African streets. Some countries, including the United States, refused to trade with South Africa. Rock stars and other famous figures spoke out against apartheid. South Africa's new president, F. W. de Klerk, realized that change was necessary. He began working to repeal the apartheid laws. In 1992, black South Africans finally obtained their full rights and freedoms.

NELSON MANDELA

Black activist Nelson Mandela devoted his life to ending apartheid. Mandela was born in Umtata, South Africa, in 1918. As a young lawyer, he helped lead the African National Congress, a group opposed to apartheid. Because he opposed the white government, in 1964 Mandela was sentenced to life in prison.

Nelson Mandela became a worldwide symbol of the injustice of apartheid. Foreign governments demanded his release. In 1990, President F. W. de Klerk agreed. Mandela and de Klerk worked together to end apartheid peacefully. They received the Nobel Peace Prize in 1993. A year later, Nelson Mandela became South Africa's first black president.

HIV/AIDS in Sports

In the early 1990s, Americans were just beginning to realize how many people were infected with HIV, the virus that causes AIDS. Several famous athletes revealed that they had the disease. Among them were Arthur Ashe, Magic Johnson, and Greg Louganis.

Arthur Ashe was a tennis player from Virginia. He was the first African-American man to win a major tennis title. During his career he won many events, including Wimbledon and the U.S. Open. Ashe probably became infected with HIV when he received tainted blood during heart surgery. In 1992, he revealed that he had AIDS. Ashe spoke publicly about the plight of people suffering from AIDS until he died in 1993 at age forty-nine.

Earvin "Magic" Johnson was one of the best professional basketball players. During the 1980s, he led the Los Angeles Lakers to five NBA titles. In 1991, the thirty-two-year-old Johnson learned that he had HIV. He retired from basketball but later returned briefly. Johnson went on to become an activist for HIV/AIDS awareness.

Arthur Ashe (1943-1993) waves to the crowd at the U.S. Open tennis tournament in August 1992. During his lifetime, Ashe used his fame to raise awareness of discrimination against African Americans.

Basketball star Magic Johnson (left) poses for a photo at a 1996 benefit for the American Foundation for AIDS Research (AmFAR). With him are (from left) Mickey Rooney, Sharon Stone, and Dr. Matilde Krim.

Greg Louganis was born in 1960 in California. As a boy, he studied dance and gymnastics. Then he switched to diving. At the 1984 Olympics, Louganis won two gold medals for diving. He repeated this feat at the 1988 Olympics. In 1995, Louganis wrote an autobiography. In the book, he revealed that he was infected with HIV.

Greg Louganis promotes his book *Breaking the Surface*, 1995. In the book, the Olympic diving star revealed that he was infected with HIV.

Workers with the International Commission on Missing Persons dug up a mass grave near Srebrenica, Bosnia and Herzegovina. One of the worst massacres of the Bosnian genocide occurred at Srebrenica in July 1995. When Serb forces captured the town, they murdered approximately seven thousand Muslim men and boys.

Mass Murder in Bosnia and Rwanda

Genocide is the planned destruction of an entire group of people. Those who commit genocide seek to wipe out people of a certain race, religion, or culture. During the 1990s, the world witnessed two separate acts of genocide.

UN peacekeeping troops on patrol in Sarajevo, 1994. The United Nations had sent peacekeepers to Bosnia and Herzegovina in 1992. However, the troops were unable to prevent conflict between Bosnian Serbs, Croats, and Muslims.

The first act of genocide took place in southeastern Europe. In the early 1990s, the country of Yugoslavia broke apart into five smaller nations. Bosnia and Herzegovina was one of the newly independent nations. Three major groups lived in Bosnia: Serbs, Croats, and Bosnian Muslims, known as Bosniaks. Members of these three ethnic groups distrusted each other. They fought for control of the new government. Before long, Bosnia erupted into civil war.

The war in Bosnia quickly turned brutal. When Serb soldiers captured a town or city, they terrorized the people living there. The soldiers wanted to get rid of anyone who was not part of their ethnic group. They put unwanted people in prison camps. They set fire to homes, churches, and mosques. Tens of thousands of Bosniak prisoners were tortured and killed. This cruel practice was called "ethnic cleansing."

The ethnic cleansing went on for over three years. More than half of Bosnia's citizens fled their homes. They became refugees. Finally, in 1995, the warring groups agreed to a peace treaty. Soldiers from other countries, including the United States, went to Bosnia to keep the peace.

An even greater tragedy occurred in Africa. Rwanda is a small country in the center of Africa. Rwanda's population is divided between two ethnic groups: the majority Hutu and the minority Tutsi. Historically, there were many clashes between members of these two groups.

Victims of the genocide in Rwanda, 1994.

Rwandan Tutsi children who escaped the violence in their home villages stand together in a UN camp for refugees, July 1994.

In 1990, a Tutsi rebel group began fighting Rwanda's government. That conflict appeared to be settled in 1993, when Rwanda's Hutu president agreed to share power with the Tutsis. In April 1994, however, the president was killed when his plane was shot down. Immediately afterward, Hutus in Rwanda—army troops, members of Hutu militia groups, and ordinary citizens alike—began killing Tutsis, as well as Hutus who supported the Tutsis.

In just one hundred days, approximately eight hundred thousand people were murdered. The genocide finally ended in July, when the Tutsi rebels took the capital city of Kigali and the Rwandan government fled.

United Nations peacekeeping troops were in Bosnia and Rwanda when the genocides took place. But in both cases, the UN failed to give the peacekeepers authority to use force to stop the killing.

TERROR BOMBING IN OKLAHOMA CITY

In 1995, a massive bomb exploded in Oklahoma City. It destroyed a government building and killed many people. It was clearly an act of terrorism. Yet it was not the work of a foreign enemy. Americans were shocked to learn that a U.S. citizen had set the bomb.

Timothy McVeigh was born in New York in 1968. As a young man, McVeigh joined the army. He served honorably in the Gulf War of 1991. After leaving the military, McVeigh became restless. He quit his job and wandered around the country.

McVeigh was not happy about the U.S. government. He believed that it robbed people of their freedom. Quietly, Timothy McVeigh planned an attack on the government. He built a bomb and placed it inside a rental truck. On the morning of April 19, 1995, he parked the truck outside the Alfred P. Murrah Federal Building in Oklahoma City.

This aerial view shows the damage caused to the Alfred P. Murrah Federal Building in Oklahoma City.

Oklahoma City firefighters help a survivor of the explosion at the Murrah building, April 1995.

McVeigh lit the bomb's fuse and quickly walked away. The blast killed 168 people and wounded hundreds more.

Timothy McVeigh was caught soon after the bombing. He was convicted and was executed for his crime in 2001. Terry Nichols, a friend who had helped McVeigh build the bomb, was also convicted. Nichols was sent to prison for life.

Police and FBI agents escort Timothy McVeigh (center) out of a courthouse two days after the Oklahoma City bombing. McVeigh was convicted in 1997, and was executed for his crimes in 2001.

Terror Bombing in Oklahoma City

O.J. SIMPSON MURDER TRIAL

*M*urder trials often attract public interest. If a celebrity is involved, the trial is sure to make news headlines. In 1995, a famous football player went on trial. He was accused of two murders. His name was O. J. Simpson.

During the 1960s and 1970s, O. J. Simpson had been an outstanding college and professional football player. After he retired from the NFL, Simpson

Police cars follow a white Ford Bronco carrying O.J. Simpson down a Los Angeles highway, June 17, 1994. The slow-speed chase was broadcast nationally while it was occurring. Simpson, who was suspected of murdering his former wife, turned himself in at the end of the chase.

O.J. Simpson (left) hired some of the country's best defense lawyers to represent him during his murder trial. They included Johnnie Cochran Jr. (center) and Robert Shapiro (right).

became an actor and TV announcer. In 1992, Simpson and his wife, Nicole Brown, were divorced. Two years later, Nicole Brown and a friend named Ronald Goldman were found stabbed to death outside Brown's home in Los Angeles. The police charged O. J. Simpson with the murders.

Simpson's trial began in January 1995. It aired live on national television. A large amount of evidence pointed to Simpson's guilt. However, his lawyers raised doubts about the evidence. They accused the Los Angeles Police Department (the same police force that had been involved in the Rodney King beating) of racial bias. They said LAPD officers had planted evidence to frame Simpson, an African-American. In October 1995, the jury found O. J. Simpson not guilty.

Simpson's legal worries were not over. The victims' families sued him in civil court (which is different from criminal court). In 1997, the civil court found Simpson responsible for the deaths. He was ordered to pay millions of dollars in damages to the family of Ronald Goldman.

A man holds a Pasadena, California, newspaper announcing the verdict in the Simpson trial. Many African Americans were happy about the verdict, because they felt that white Los Angeles police officers had tried to frame Simpson.

Music Goes Grunge and Hip-Hop

Two different types of music ruled the 1990s. Grunge evolved from punk music and heavy metal. Hip-hop grew out of the rap music of the 1980s. Fans of grunge and hip-hop each built a culture around their music.

Grunge music started in Seattle, Washington. The bands Nirvana and Pearl Jam came from this city. So did Soundgarden and Alice in Chains. These groups

Kurt Cobain (left), Dave Grohl (drums), and Krist Novoselic (right) of Nirvana perform on MTV, 1993. Nirvana was one of the most popular grunge bands of the 1990s.

created a unique sound. They used heavy guitar riffs and dark, gloomy lyrics. Grunge fans did not want to be flashy. They dressed in flannel shirts and ripped jeans. In 1994, Nirvana singer Kurt Cobain killed himself. In the years afterward, the popularity of grunge music began to decline.

Hip-hop moved in two directions during the 1990s. Gangsta rap stressed the violent side of city life. Artists rapped about street gangs, drive-by shootings, and police brutality. Ice Cube and Ice-T were two early gangsta rappers. Other hip-hop artists rejected gangsta culture. Performers such as Will Smith and LL Cool J scored hits with more upbeat themes. Hip-hop fans of the 1990s liked baggy jeans and sports jerseys. They wore their baseball caps sideways. Hip-hop music and culture remains popular today.

Lauryn Hill was one of the most successful hip-hop artists of the 1990s. Her 1998 album *The Miseducation of Lauryn Hill* sold more than ten million copies and won five Grammy Awards.

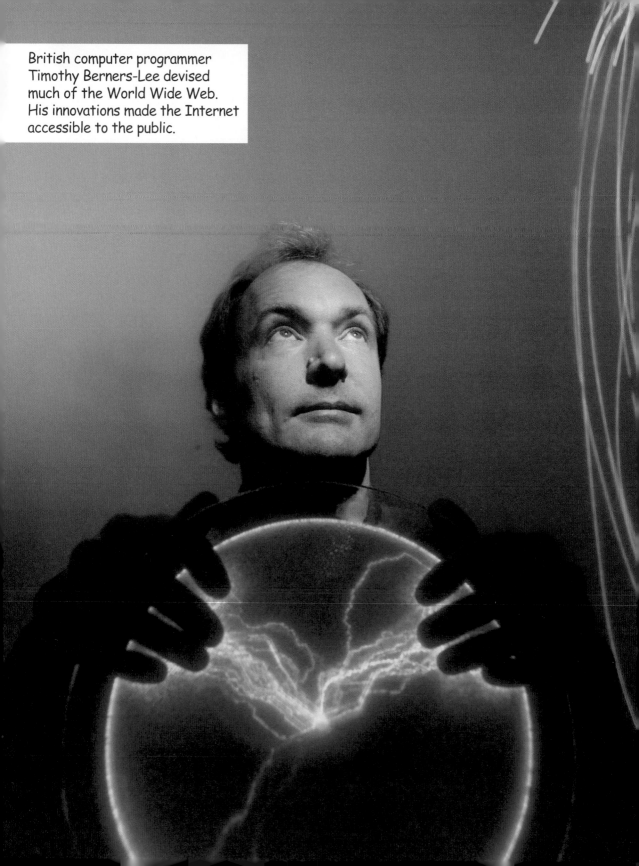

British computer programmer Timothy Berners-Lee devised much of the World Wide Web. His innovations made the Internet accessible to the public.

RISE OF THE INTERNET

*T*oday it is hard to imagine life without the Internet. The vast computer network connects computers from all across the globe. We use it for work, for entertainment, and to talk with others. Yet the Internet is a relatively new invention. It only became widely available in the mid-1990s.

Scientists working for the U.S. Department of Defense began building a computer network in the late 1960s. They needed to work together across long distances. The scientists found a way to link their computers. They swapped data via telephone lines and cables. At first, the public had little access to the network, which was called ARPANET (Advanced Research Projects

During the late 1960s, Vinton Cerf worked on the ARPANET project. He helped create a way for computers to communicate over telephone lines, called the Transmission Control Protocol/Internet Protocol (TCP/IP). Because of his work, Cerf has often been called "father of the Internet."

Agency Network). However, during the 1980s, growing numbers of people began purchasing personal computers. Some began connecting to ARPANET through what were called bulletin-board systems, or BBSs.

In 1989, a British scientist named Timothy Berners-Lee invented the World Wide Web. It added pictures and sound to the text-only Internet. Using Berners-Lee's system, users could perform a search and click on links to visit other sites. By 1993, programs called browsers were making the Web easily accessible to everyone. Before long, millions of people were going online. They hailed the Internet as the "information superhighway."

In 1998, Apple introduced the iMac, a personal computer that could easily be connected to the Internet. The brightly colored computers quickly became popular in homes and schools.

Computer company owner Michael Dell was one of the first businesspeople to recognize the sales potential of the Internet. Dell Computer launched its Web site in June 1994. Within two years, the company was earning more than $1 million a day just through Internet sales.

The Internet made communication easier. With e-mail, users could keep in touch with faraway friends and relatives. Chat rooms enabled people to make new friends around the world. Online clubs and discussion groups formed. Search engines such as Yahoo! and Google became instant hits. They helped people find Web sites of interest. Some users learned how to create their own sites. They began posting their thoughts and ideas in online diaries called Web logs, or "blogs."

Many companies built Web sites to sell their products. Amazon.com was among the first. It began selling books online in 1995. Amazon and companies like it showed the business power of the Web. A regular bookstore could only attract customers who lived nearby. An online bookstore like Amazon was different. It sold products to customers from around the globe.

The Internet also gave society new problems. Hackers learned how to steal private information from people's computers. Thieves used this information to break into online bank accounts. Some users downloaded copies of songs and movies without paying for them. Worst of all, violent criminals began using the Internet to find unsuspecting new victims. People quickly learned to avoid giving personal information online.

In 1981, just 213 computers were connected to the Internet. By the end of the 1990s, that number had grown to more than 400 million. Today, over a billion people use the Internet each day. It has become an essential tool for work, fun, and shopping. It can also be a great source of information for students doing research, although not all Web sites are reliable.

EXPLORING SPACE

*T*echnology in the 1990s made it possible to study space like never before. The Hubble Space Telescope revealed distant secrets of the universe. Meanwhile, the *Mars Pathfinder* probed the surface of another planet. These two machines led scientists to amazing new discoveries.

Since being launched into orbit, the Hubble Space Telescope has taken many pictures of distant galaxies. The colored lines are bits of a star that exploded in the Large Magellanic Cloud galaxy.

Unlike other telescopes, Hubble orbits the Earth. It is outside of Earth's atmosphere. This enables Hubble to get a much clearer view of the universe than ground-based telescopes, because Earth's atmosphere distorts and blocks light that reaches the planet.

Hubble was launched in 1990. It did not work properly at first. Scientists found a flaw in one of the telescope's delicate mirrors. In 1993, astronauts fixed the problem. Since then, Hubble has recorded brilliant images of distant stars and planets. Thanks to the Hubble Space Telescope, scientists now believe that there are about 125 billion galaxies in the universe.

The *Mars Pathfinder* landed on Mars on July 4, 1997. It beamed back stunning pictures of the Martian landscape. *Pathfinder* then released a small, six-wheeled vehicle called *Sojourner*. Scientists on Earth steered the rover by remote control. They used it to study Martian rocks and soil. For three months, *Pathfinder* and *Sojourner* sent back valuable data about Mars. Their mission ended in October 1997 when their batteries finally died.

Exploring Space

ERA OF THE SITCOM

*T*he word *sitcom* is short for "situation comedy." A sitcom is a type of
television show. In each episode, the characters are placed in funny
situations. There were many sitcoms in the 1990s. Three of the most popular
were *Seinfeld*, *Friends*, and *The Simpsons*.

Seinfeld was based on the real-life observations of comedian Jerry Seinfeld.
Each week, Jerry and his three friends dealt with everyday problems that

This scene in Jerry Seinfeld's apartment features the show's four stars.
Pictured are (left to right) Julia Louis-Dreyfus, Jerry Seinfeld, Michael
Richards, and Jason Alexander.

The cast of the television show *Friends* included (front, left to right) Jennifer Aniston, Matthew Perry, Matt LeBlanc, (back) David Schwimmer, Courteney Cox, and Lisa Kudrow.

viewers found humorous. Many scenes took place in Jerry's tiny apartment. Viewers enjoyed the show's witty jokes and clever plots. *Seinfeld* ran for nine seasons before finishing in 1998.

Friends first aired in 1994. The show was about six young men and women trying to succeed in New York City. *Friends* was an instant hit. Young adult viewers identified with the group's amusing dilemmas. The six cast members became celebrities. They went on to star in movies and other TV shows. Over 50 million people watched the final episode of *Friends* in 2004.

The Simpsons is the longest-running sitcom ever. It debuted in 1989. At the time, the idea of an animated sitcom was unique. However, the Simpson family became part of American culture. Their antics kept viewers laughing through the 1990s and beyond.

IDO GONZALEZ   SHARON STONE   MODE

AFSANE BASSIR POUR

HIV/AIDS
RAVAGES AFRICA

During the 1980s, Americans became aware of a deadly disease called acquired immunodeficiency syndrome, or AIDS. Scientists discovered that this disease was caused by a virus. They named it the human immunodeficiency virus, or HIV. During the 1990s, HIV/AIDS became a major health crisis in Africa. It still ravages Africa today.

HIV makes a person's body unable to fight off other diseases. As a result, AIDS patients often suffer from many illnesses. Over time, these illnesses combine to weaken the patient, who usually dies. There are three ways that a person can get HIV. One way is through contact with infected blood (for example, by sharing a contaminated hypodermic needle). Another way is by having sex with an infected partner. Lastly, an infected mother may pass the virus on to her baby.

HIV/AIDS has affected nearly every nation in the world. The disease strikes hardest in poor countries. Those nations do not have the means to cope with it. Their governments are weak and face many other problems. Health care is limited. People have little education and may not know how to avoid infection. The disease thrives in these conditions. About 95 percent of all HIV-infected people live in poor countries.

Africa quickly became the center of the HIV/AIDS epidemic. The continent has long struggled with poverty, war, and corruption. In the 1990s, the disease spread out of control in Africa. Many African governments were slow to teach

American actress Sharon Stone (center), representing the American Foundation for AIDS Research (AmFAR), speaks to the United Nations on World AIDS Day, 1998. By the end of the 1990s, about 22 million Africans were HIV-positive.

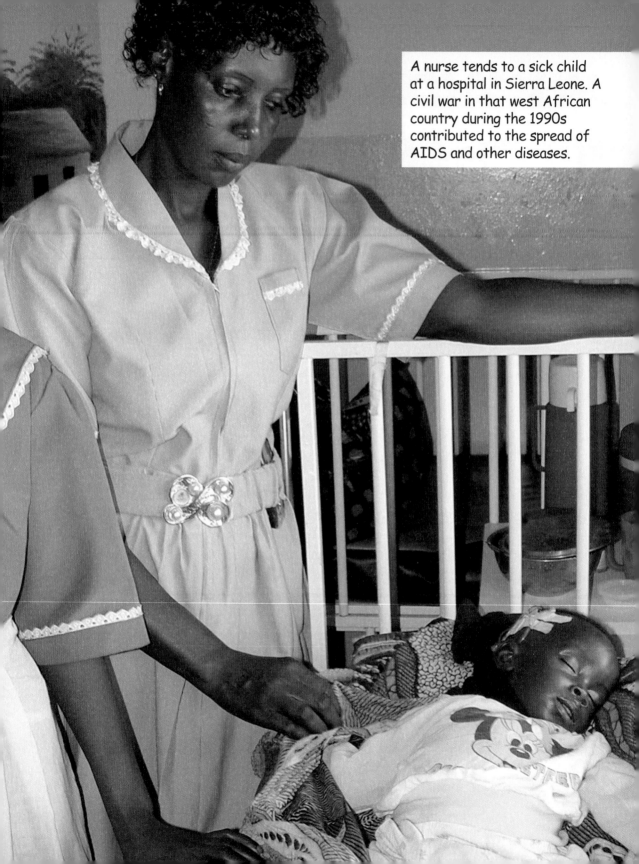

A nurse tends to a sick child at a hospital in Sierra Leone. A civil war in that west African country during the 1990s contributed to the spread of AIDS and other diseases.

their citizens how to protect themselves from HIV. The virus spread rapidly. Infected women often gave birth to infected babies.

Today, African governments are working hard to slow the spread of the virus. Nations from around the globe are helping them. Yet progress is slow. Roughly 7,000 new infections occur each day in Africa. Seven out of every ten HIV/AIDS victims come from that continent. The virus has helped shorten the average life span in Africa. In several African nations, the average person now dies around age 40.

As young adults grow ill and die from the disease, Africa's problems worsen. More children are becoming orphans. Some regions face a shortage of workers. There are not enough farmers to grow food. Schools have too few teachers. The effects of HIV/AIDS will continue to be felt in Africa for decades to come.

A woman speaks about how to prevent AIDS at a meeting in Bangui, Central African Republic. Since the 1990s, many international organizations have worked with African governments to educate Africans about HIV infection.

AL-QAEDA BOMBS U.S. EMBASSIES

In 1998, the terrorist organization al-Qaeda staged a pair of deadly attacks against American targets. Two U.S. embassies in Africa were bombed.

An embassy is a building in a foreign country where diplomats work. The diplomats represent their nation to the host country. Al-Qaeda attacked the

Africans help rescue one of the people injured when a bomb exploded near the U.S. embassy in Nairobi, Kenya, on August 7, 1998.

U.S. Secretary of Defense William S. Cohen (left) and General Henry H. Shelton discuss the August 20, 1998, military strike that destroyed terrorist training camps in Afghanistan. A second cruise missile attack destroyed a factory in Sudan that American leaders suspected was used to make chemical weapons.

U.S. embassies in Kenya and Tanzania. The two attacks happened at almost the exact same time on August 7, 1998. Powerful blasts rocked both buildings. The Kenya bomb killed 213 people. Twelve were Americans. The rest were Kenyans who worked in and around the embassy. Eleven people died in the Tanzania blast. Both explosions injured many innocent bystanders.

President Bill Clinton wanted to punish al-Qaeda for the embassy attacks. Yet he did not wish to risk the lives of U.S. soldiers. He decided to strike al-Qaeda camps with cruise missiles. The unmanned missiles hit targets in Sudan and Afghanistan. They did little meaningful damage, however.

A Saudi billionaire and radical Muslim named Osama bin Laden organized the 1998 al-Qaeda attacks on the American embassies. Two years earlier, bin Laden had publicly committed his followers to war against the United States.

THE MAGIC OF HARRY POTTER

A new book thrilled British readers in 1997. Author J. K. Rowling wrote the story of a young wizard named Harry Potter, who attended the Hogwarts School of Witchcraft and Wizardry. Before long, people all over the world were reading about Harry's adventures.

A nine-year-old girl poses with her copy of *Harry Potter and the Goblet of Fire* at a bookstore in Texas. The Harry Potter books were first published in the United Kingdom. By the late 1990s, young American readers had become aware of the stories.

Harry Potter and the Sorcerer's Stone was one of the best-selling novels of all time. The story charmed readers of all ages. They enjoyed the magical world of Harry and his friends. J. K. Rowling wrote six more Harry Potter books. They too became best sellers. Hollywood began making the books into movies.

The Harry Potter books have sold more than 400 million copies. They have been printed in 67 languages. The Harry Potter series still enchants readers today.

Author J. K. Rowling

J. K. Rowling began writing stories at age six. However, she did not find success as a writer until she was thirty-two years old. In the mid-1990s, Rowling had no job and little money. She was raising a small child alone. Yet she refused to give up on her writing. Rowling had an idea for a book about a boy wizard. She named him Harry Potter. She wrote the first novel in cafés while her daughter slept beside her. Today, J. K. Rowling is an extremely wealthy celebrity.

J. K. Rowling has won many awards for her seven books about the wizard Harry Potter and his friends.

School Shooting at Columbine

In April 1999, two teens attacked their classmates and teachers. They used guns and bombs. The attack occurred at Columbine High School in Colorado. When it was over, thirteen victims and the two attackers lay dead. More than twenty others were wounded. It was one of the deadliest school shootings in U.S. history.

Students escape from gunmen at Columbine High School in Littleton, Colorado.

Columbine students Eric Harris (left) and Dylan Klebold appear in this surveillance videotape of the school's cafeteria. Harris and Klebold murdered twelve other students and a teacher, then killed themselves.

The two young men, Eric Harris and Dylan Klebold, launched their assault on the morning of April 20, 1999. They walked through the school, shooting at students and teachers. They also threw pipe bombs. Their rampage lasted more than 45 minutes. As police closed in, the attackers committed suicide.

The Columbine massacre shocked the nation. It prompted many debates about American society and the safety of public schools. People tried to understand the attackers' motives. They also wondered how two youths could acquire such powerful weapons. Investigators learned that the young men had a dark history. They had been arrested for theft. Violent video games, films, and music fascinated them. At school, they had been bullied. They resented athletes and popular students.

After the Columbine tragedy, schools across the country added more security. Counselors reached out to troubled students. Teachers cracked down on bullying. Idle threats of violence were taken more seriously. Despite these steps, there would be a number of school shootings after Columbine.

Mourners visit a memorial for the victims of the Columbine school shooting, April 1999.

Getting Ready for Y2K

As the 1990s neared an end, a problem emerged. It had to do with computers. People had come to rely on computers for many tasks. Computer programs ran traffic lights and telephones. They assisted airplane pilots. They helped to generate and distribute electricity. They kept track of bank accounts and financial records. However, nobody was sure that all of the computers would still work properly in the year 2000. They were afraid of a computer glitch that became known as the Year 2000 problem, or simply Y2K.

President Clinton discusses the Y2K problem at the National Academy of Science. Many people feared that a software glitch would cause huge problems for businesses and the government.

Some families prepared for Y2K by hoarding food and stockpiling wood to burn for heat. People also purchased power generators that ran on diesel fuel or gasoline in case the electrical grid shut down because of the computer problem.

The Y2K problem rested with older computer programs. To save space, early programmers had used only two digits to represent the year. (For example, 1968 was stored only as "68" in older computer systems.) Since 2000 would appear as "00," people worried that computers might mistake the year 2000 with 1900. If so, important programs might stop working. Governments warned citizens to prepare for possible disaster. At the same time, programmers everywhere scrambled to fix the Y2K problem before January 1, 2000.

They succeeded. New Year's Day passed without incident. Some minor computer glitches did occur around the world, but they caused little harm and were quickly fixed. The Y2K scare was over.

LOOKING AHEAD

As clocks ticked toward midnight on December 31, 1999, the anticipation grew. All over the world, people gathered with friends, neighbors, or crowds of complete strangers to welcome the start of a new millennium. In cities and towns on every continent, huge celebrations marked the occasion.

The joyful mood would not last very long. Old problems do not go away simply because the calendar changes. For years, American politics had been bitterly divided between Democrats and Republicans, liberals and conservatives. That bitterness would reach new levels during the presidential election of 2000. The election was one of the most controversial in U.S. history—and it would only be decided by one of the most controversial Supreme Court decisions in history.

The new president, George W. Bush, soon faced a severe test. On September 11, 2001, al-Qaeda terrorists killed nearly 3,000 Americans with hijacked airplanes. The president responded by ordering an invasion of Afghanistan, whose government was sheltering al-Qaeda members. The Bush administration also used the September 11 attacks to justify an invasion of Iraq in 2003. Eventually, that decision would prove very unpopular. But it was just one of the reasons the American people grew angry with the Republican president, and with the Republicans in Congress who supported his policies.

Democrats did very well in the 2008 elections. They picked up seats in the Senate and House of Representatives. Most notably, however, a Democrat who promised change won the presidency and made history. As the first decade of the new millennium came to a close, the United States was led by Barack Obama—the nation's first African-American president.

On January 20, 2009, Barack Obama became the first African-American president of the United States. Here, the new president dances with his wife, Michelle, during an inauguration event.

CHRONOLOGY

1990—The Human Genome Project begins. Iraq invades Kuwait in August. Iraqi leader Saddam Hussein ignores worldwide demands to withdraw his troops. Forces from more than thirty nations gather in nearby Saudi Arabia.

1991—The Gulf War starts in January. Kuwait is freed in February. Basketball star Magic Johnson reveals that he has HIV / AIDS.

1992—In April, the Rodney King case sparks a race riot in Los Angeles. Bill Clinton is elected president in November. Apartheid ends in South Africa.

1993—Ramzi Yousef sets off a bomb beneath the World Trade Center in February. It kills six people, but fails to topple the twin towers. Tennis champion Arthur Ashe dies from HIV / AIDS.

1994—The Rwandan genocide begins in April. Singer Kurt Cobain of the grunge band Nirvana commits suicide. Nelson Mandela becomes South Africa's first black president. The sitcom *Friends* debuts on television.

1995—In April, Timothy McVeigh blows up a government building in Oklahoma City. Retired football player O. J. Simpson is acquitted of murder charges in October. Online shopping becomes popular with the launch of eBay and Amazon.com.

1996—Scottish scientists clone a sheep, which they name Dolly. In November, Bill Clinton is reelected president.

1997—The first Harry Potter book is released in England. In July, *Pathfinder* lands on the surface of Mars.

1998—The final episode of the sitcom *Seinfeld* airs in May. In August, al-Qaeda bombs two U.S. embassies in Africa. America responds with cruise missile attacks in Sudan and Afghanistan.

1999—In April, two students go on a deadly shooting rampage at Columbine High School in Colorado. Programmers rush to fix the Y2K computer glitch before January 1, 2000.

GLOSSARY

al-Qaeda—A terrorist group responsible for many attacks, including the 9/11 attacks.

apartheid—A policy of racial separation and discrimination against blacks in South Africa that ended in the 1990s.

clone—In science, to create an exact copy of a plant or animal.

coalition—A temporary alliance of people or nations.

epidemic—The widespread outbreak of a disease.

ethnic—Referring to a group's race, religion, or culture.

genocide—The planned destruction of an ethnic group.

HIV/AIDS—A disease that weakens the body's ability to fight off other diseases.

massacre—The act of killing a large number of people.

network—A system of computers connected to share data.

rampage—A series of violent and frenzied actions.

refugee—A person who flees to find safety from a war or other disaster.

sitcom—Short for situation comedy, it is a type of television show.

technology—Society's use of tools and science.

terrorism—The use of violence and fear to achieve political goals.

Further Reading

Bobek, Milan, editor. *Decades of the Twentieth Century: The 1990s*. Pittsburgh, Pa.: Eldorado Ink, 2005.

Brown, Laaren, and Lenny Hort. *Nelson Mandela*. New York: DK Publishing, 2006.

Brownell, Richard. *The Oklahoma City Bombing*. Farmington Hills, Mich.: Lucent Books, 2007.

Carruthers, Margaret W. *The Hubble Space Telescope*. New York: Franklin Watts, 2003.

Gelletly, Leeanne. *Africa: Progress & Problems: AIDS and Health Issues*. Philadelphia, Pa.: Mason Crest Publishers, 2006.

Morgan, Sally. *From Sea Urchins to Dolly the Sheep: Discovering Cloning*. Chicago, Ill.: Heinemann, 2006.

Rice Jr., Earle. *Overview of the Persian Gulf War*. Hockessin, Del.: Mitchell Lane Publishers, 2008.

Sammartino McPherson, Stephanie. *Bill Clinton*. Minneapolis, Minn.: Lerner Publishing Group, 2008.

Spalding, Frank. *Genocide in Rwanda*. New York: Rosen Publishing, 2008.

Internet Resources

<http://www.un.org/av/photo/subjects/apartheid.htm>
The United Nations presents this photo-filled history of apartheid in South Africa.

<http://www.oklahomacitynationalmemorial.org/>
The Oklahoma City National Memorial honors those who died in the 1995 bombing. This official site offers a compelling study of the tragedy.

<http://mpfwww.jpl.nasa.gov/funzone_flash.html>
Learn more about the exploration of Mars at this NASA site. It includes games and instructions for building a model of the *Mars Pathfinder*.

INDEX

PICTURE CREDITS

Illustration credits: AP/Wide World Photos: 6, 7, 30, 31 (top), 33 (bottom), 51 (bottom), 53 (bottom); courtesy of Dell, Inc.: 39; FilmMagic: 34; Getty Images: 19 (top), 25 (top), 26, 32, 36, 37, 50, 53 (top), 54; AFP/Getty Images: 9, 13 (bottom), 19 (bottom), 31 (bottom), 33 (top), 48, 49 (bottom), 52; Time & Life Pictures/Getty Images: 12, 14, 25 (bottom), 35 (top), 55; © The State of Israel: 5; © 2009 Jupiterimages Corporation: 16, 18; NBC-TV/the Kobal Collection: 42; Warner Bros TV/Bright Kauffman Crane Productions/the Kobal Collection: 43; Landov: 13 (top); Reuters/Mike Segar/Landov: 17; Reuters/Ray Stubblebine/Landov: 1 (bottom right), 24; Library of Congress: 1 (top), 14; National Aeronautics and Space Administration: 40, 41; PhotoFest: 51 (top); Redferns: 35 (bottom); used under license from Shutterstock, Inc.: 4; Stockbyte: 1 (bottom left), 38; United Nations photo: 20, 21, 22, 23, 27, 29, 44, 47; L. Lartigue/USAID: 46; U.S. Department of Defense: 8, 10, 11, 28, 49 (top), 57.

Cover photos: Reuters/Ray Stubblebine/Landov (Arthur Ashe); Library of Congress (Clinton inauguration); Stockbyte (students at computers).